BOTANICAL INSPIRATION

20th Anniviction:ary

Published and distributed by
viction:workshop ltd.

viction:ary™

viction:workshop ltd.
Unit C, 7/F, Seabright Plaza,
9-23 Shell Street, North Point, Hong Kong
Url: www.victionary.com
Email: we@victionary.com
🅕 @victionworkshop
🅞 @victionworkshop
Bē @victionary
🅟 @victionary

Edited & produced by viction:ary

Creative direction by Victor Cheung
Book design by viction:workshop ltd.
Showcase & quote typeface: Ogg by Sharp Type
Endpaper image: A Secular Gathering by Karin Miller

Third Edition

ISBN 978-988-79034-9-9
Printed and bound in China

BOTANICAL INSPIRATION

NATURE IN ART & ILLUSTRATION

PREFACE

BY VICTION:ARY

As a publisher of books on design, art, and illustration for the past 20 years, we have had the privilege of showcasing various creative talents from all over the world who specialise in a multitude of subjects, skills, and mediums. In doing so, we have found that while every project stands out in its own distinct way, there are also fundamental concepts or elements that connect one piece of work with another – making their creators kindred spirits of sorts through the source(s) of inspiration from which they draw their magic and meaning.

After releasing Flora & Fauna, our best-selling book on design inspired by nature in the spring of 2019, we felt that it was only natural to follow it up with a curation of art and illustration work on plants. To us, Botanical Inspiration is not just about riding the ever-growing trend of slow-living in a hectic modern age, or weighing in on the bohemian 'jungalow' aesthetic that has grown in popularity today. Although many things have and will continue to transform as is expected of the circle of life, this book hopes to bear testament to the fact that even amidst impending tides of change, some creative ideas will always remain timelessly appealing, and in spite of our individual circumstances, we all instinctively respond the strongest to what surrounds and connects us.

Besides having the same underlying theme, the artists and illustrators in this book have interpreted their own botanical inspirations in visual and visceral ways that intertwine via intention or approach. Keen observers and painters Yuko Kurihara (p.256) and Anna Valdez (p.154) demonstrate their knack for eye-catching colour combinations in framing the extraordinary beauty of ordinary objects and the everyday through their vibrant still-lifes. Similarly, artist Dana Kinter (p.246) gives prominence to the delicate details that usually pass us by, but with more organic line-work and a muted palette.

Illustrators like Clover Robin (p.146) and Lili Arnold (p.240) are successful in applying their personal styles to practical purposes such as book covers and textiles. Whether it is Clover's collages or Lili's block prints, their craft adds new dimensions to the canvas to resonate with a wider audience by telling stories of their own. Karin Miller (p.136) and Tiffany Bozic (p.074), on the other hand, create fantastical and fairy-tale-like wonderlands with surrealistic elements to take their viewers into imaginary realms. For work that brims with raw character, Julia Lucey (p.058) and Agathe Singer (p.186) are among the many who explore the limitless possibilities of expression and techniques like etching and gouache to stunning effect.

As much as this book celebrates creativity as diverse as nature itself, Botanical Inspiration is also dedicated to the very life force that unifies us on this planet. Whether you are a creative professional or someone who just loves to stop and smell the roses, we hope that these pages will at the very least inspire you to take in all that surrounds you with a new sense of wonder and feel the joy in simply being alive.

"Beauty surrounds us, but usually we need to be walking in a garden to know it." — Rumi

FOREWORD

BY SENAKA SENANAYAKE

Beauty has often been depicted as flora and fauna since time immemorial. They are a testimony of nature's creations and celebrate her splendour. For artists who paint beauty, there cannot be a better muse. As beacons of life and its fragility, they offer hope and inspiration to humans across the world.

I started painting at the early age of eight and had my first solo exhibition when I was ten. Upon completing my formal education at Yale in the US and eventually returning to Sri Lanka, I was compelled to paint more profusely; making the latter country's inhabitants, celebrations, as well as flora and fauna that existed in abundance my muse. Verdant rainforests once covered my island nation, and even though development had already claimed large tracts of them at the time, I wanted to capture all that I could.

Looking back even further into my past, I have always been drawn to flora, as many dotted the garden of my childhood home. Whether it was a ginger flower's bloom or the incandescent light of a moonlit lotus, they all found and formed a keen observer in me. To this day, I still visit the Sri Lankan rainforests as well as places like the Singapore Botanic Gardens just to take in nature's marvels. In fact, my trip to the former often inspires me to paint its beauty in all its glory.

Whether it is the dozen types of blossoms or the different hues of banana groves, I borrow elements from nature's arbour and rearrange them on my canvas to bring their true colours to life. Every piece of painting is a message of preservation, and its impact is not meant to be limited to a wall or the size of a device screen. Rather, let it lead you to discover more about the eco-system in which the plant thrives.

My realm of painting also abandons the age-old one of disaster and distortion. Instead, it reflects one of tolerance and balance, as ultimately, our values should never turn us against the Earth or risk its very survival. The brush is my tool for the conservation of our enchanted yet endangered lands, the iridescent colours of which could go missing from our modern world at any time.

Through my work, I hope that viewers – especially the youth – will cherish, nurture, and protect our precious habitations from a peril that could engulf us all. I do not wish to merely be archiving lost treasures like it was done in the colonial era, when the botanist was accompanied by the artist to document different plant species. Rather, let me continue to inspire; to live and let live!

As you peruse this volume dedicated to the beauty that only Mother Nature brims with, I also hope that you will come to appreciate the marvels that have been painstakingly recreated by my fellow artists, then make a pledge to let Her legacy prevail – if not for ourselves, then for the generations to come.

AN
INTRODUCTION
TO
PLANTS

Essential to our existence in every way possible, plants play an important role in enriching and ensuring the survival of our planet. The greatest thinkers and makers have often looked to them for inspiration, using them as the source and subject matter of creative expressions due not only to the countless possibilities that their sheer variety presents, but also the pure and simple way with which the smallest of elements can touch the soul. In all their shapes, shades, and sizes, plants are truly nature's palette and will continue to be inherent to our creativity as long as the Earth thrives. Although nobody knows for sure just how many species there are in total today, new ones are discovered around the world every year, providing humankind with more symbols of hope, growth, and joy. From a biological standpoint, botanists generally group plants into the vascular and non-vascular – both of which can be further classified into four categories: bryophytes, pteridophytes, gymnosperms, and angiosperms. In terms of characteristics, each category is determined by the plants' ability to transport water and bear seeds, among other criteria.

I. BRYOPHYTES

Considered by scientists to be the earliest plants on the planet, non-vascular plants are those that lack vessels or tissues that can transport nutrients from the ground. Bryophytes fall under this unique group and are actually found all around us, but because they lack leaves, stems, and roots, plants in this category are typically overlooked or ignored. Commonly known as mosses, liverworts, or hornworts, they live in moist places or relatively dry environments like sandy soils due to their non-existent structural support, getting however much moisture from the air as they can to absorb the minerals they need to survive. Although most of them may not seem appealing at first glance – for example, mosses are usually found on rotting logs – there is a distinct sense of beauty in the bryophyte texture, form, and ability to thrive in harsh conditions.

• COMMON / UMBRELLA LIVERWORT
Scientific Name: Marchantia Polymorpha

• COMMON HAIRCAP / HAIR MOSS
Scientific Name: Polytrichum Commune

• PINCUSHION MOSS
Scientific Name: Leucobryum Glaucum

• BONFIRE MOSS
Scientific Name: Funaria Hygrometrica

• FLOATING CRYSTALWORT
Scientific Name: Riccia Fluitans

• SILVERY THREAD MOSS
Scientific Name: Bryum Argenteum

• JAVA MOSS
Scientific Name: Vesicular Dubyana

II. PTERIDOPHYTES

Almost 12,000 species of ferns can be categorised as pteridophytes, which fall under the vascular plants group. As the name suggests, vascular plants contain inner vessels or tissues known as xylem and phloem that help them distribute the nutrients necessary for growth. As such, they have more flexibility in terms of where their geographical or climate bases could be. In the case of pteridophytes, they are primarily forest-dwelling plants that share a distinct graceful vibe due to the delicate patterns of their leaves. Despite also being united by the fact that they produce no seeds, cones, or fruits, they are extremely diverse in terms of physical appearance and size – ranging from those of the tiny ferns floating in rice paddies to the tree ferns in tropical forests that can reach up to 30 metres in height.

• EAGLE FERN
Scientific Name: Pteridium Aquilinum

• ELKHORN / COMMON STAGHORN FERN
Scientific Name: Platycerium Bifurcatum

• BIRD'S NEST FERN
Scientific Name: Asplenium Nidus

• FIVE-FINGERED / NORTHERN MAIDENHAIR FERN
Scientific Name: Adiantum Pedatum

• THE GREAT HORSETAIL
Scientific Name: Equisetum Telmateia

• DWARF HORSETAIL
Scientific Name: Equisetum Scirpoides

III. GYMNOSPERMS

- ATLAS CEDAR
Scientific Name:
Cedrus Atlantica

- ROCKY MOUNTAIN
DOUGLAS FIR
Scientific Name:
Pseudotsuga Menziesii
Glauca

- AFRICAN CYPRESS
Scientific Name:
Widdringtonia

- CHINESE JUNIPER
Scientific Name:
Juniperus Chinensis

- BRISTLECONE PINE
Scientific Name:
Pinus Aristata

- CANARY ISLAND PINE
Scientific Name:
Pinus Canariensis

Among all the plant types, gymnosperms comprise some of the tallest, thickest, and oldest ones on the planet under the vascular plants group. Like pteridophytes (i.e. ferns) and angiosperms (i.e. flowering plants), they contain tissues that transport nutrients from the ground and help them reach their relatively large sizes. Although geographically widely distributed, commonly recognisable gymnosperms can mostly be found in the temperate and arctic regions, like the towering pine and lush firs one would expect to see on the mountains of the northern hemisphere. Although they would usually be associated with cooler climates, the gingko tree in China is often referred to as a 'living fossil' that existed nearly 200 million years ago. As a whole, gymnosperms make good sources of wood and paper.

IV. ANGIOSPERMS

- PRICKLY PEAR
Scientific Name: Opuntia

- HEDGEHOG CACTI
Scientific Name:
Echinopsis

- MEXICAN TEOSINTE
Scientific Name:
Zea Mexicana

- PERSIAN BUTTERCUP
Scientific Name:
Ranunculus Asiaticus

- WINTER CHERRY
Scientific Name:
Solanum Pseudocapsicum

- MOTH ORCHID
Scientific Name:
Phalaenopsis

- SPRENGER'S
MAGNOLIA
Scientific Name:
Magnolia Sprengeri

- COMMON
SUNFLOWER
Scientific Name:
Helianthus Annuus

The most diverse plant category in the world with over 260,000 living species found so far, angiosperms fall under the vascular plant group and are the most eye-catching, easily identifiable botanical variants due to their flowering capabilities. Their main biological make-up can be explained by the term 'angiosperm' itself, which derives from the Greek words 'angeion' referring to the vessels used for transporting nutrients, as well as 'sperma', which points to the seeds that help the plants reproduce. Each flower generally has four visible sets of organs – sepals, petals, stamens, and carpels – that help in the fruiting process. Although flowers are typically featured in creative work due to their wide range of physical characteristics, trees, herbs, shrubs, bulbs, and parasitic plants as a whole are also extremely useful as food, medicine, and sources of fibre.

OANA
BEFORT

LUCILA DOMINGUEZ

SENAKA
SENANAYAKE

I am a kind word uttered and repeated
By the voice of Nature;
I am a star fallen from the
Blue tent upon the green carpet.
I am the daughter of the elements
With whom Winter conceived;
To whom Spring gave birth; I was
Reared in the lap of Summer and I
Slept in the bed of Autumn.
At dawn I unite with the breeze
To announce the coming of light;
At eventide I join the birds
In bidding the light farewell.
The plains are decorated with
My beautiful colours, and the air
Is scented with my fragrance.

Excerpt from 'Song of the Flower XXIII'
by Khalil Gibran

2013
Senaka Senanayake

MIROCOMACHIKO

mirocomachiko

NATURE IN ART & ILLUSTRATION

035

LAURA GARCIA SERVENTI

TIFFANY KINGSTON

WHOOLI
CHEN

054

JULIA LUCEY

Nature's first green is gold,
Her hardest hue to hold.
Her early leaf's a flower;
But only so an hour.
Then leaf subsides to leaf.
So Eden sank to grief,
So dawn goes down to day.
Nothing gold can stay.

'Nothing Gold Can Stay'
by Robert Frost

ROSA DE WEERD

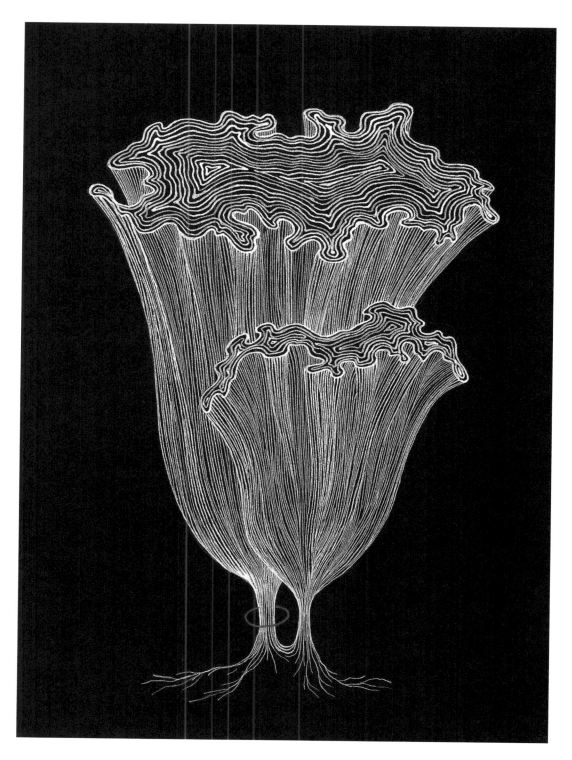

ANDREA WAN

TIFFANY
BOZIC

EDITH REWA
BARRETT

WOOLLY
STARS
OF
THE
LOWER
BUSH

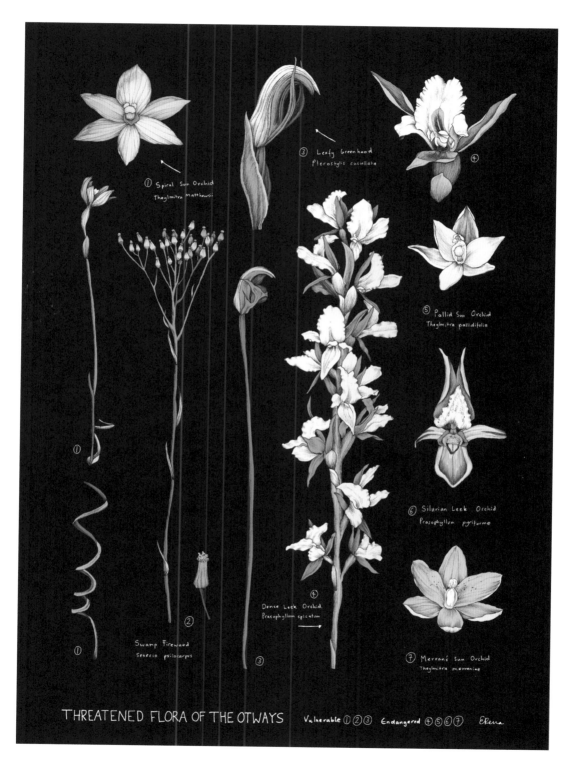

① Spiral Sun Orchid
Thelymitra Matthewsii

③ Leafy Greenhood
Pterostylis cucullata

④

⑤ Pallid Sun Orchid
Thelymitra pallidifolia

⑥ Silurian Leek Orchid
Prasophyllum pyriforme

Dense Leek Orchid
Prasophyllum spicatum

Swamp Firewood
Senecio psilocarpus

⑦ Merran's Sun Orchid
Thelymitra merraniae

THREATENED FLORA OF THE OTWAYS   Vulnerable ①②③ Endangered ④⑤⑥⑦   ERena

OANA BEFORT

oanabefort.com

Oana Befort is a Romania-born graphic artist, freelance illustrator, wife, and mother of two based in the Midwest of the US. Her mixed media illustrations are inspired by the natural world, folk motifs, flora, fauna, nostalgia, and everyday life, with a quirky and modern interpretation to them.

012 / 013 **NIGHT-BLOOMING CEREUS**
Watercolour, Gouache
280 x 355 mm

BLUE FLORA
Watercolour
280 x 355 mm

014 / 015 **MOTH & FLORA**
Watercolour, Gouache
280 x 355 mm

ROSE FLORA
Watercolour, Gouache
280 x 355 mm

016 / 017 **FLORA**
Watercolour, Gouache, Digital Collage

PEONIES
Watercolour, Gouache
280 x 355 mm

LUCILA DOMINGUEZ

lucilismo.com

Lucila Dominguez is an Buenos Aires-based artist working worldwide. Passionate about nature, she is inspired by its beauty to create her own universe which is rich with details, textures, and the delicate use of colour and light. Her paintings are joyful and expressive with hints of mystery and surrealism.

018 / 019 **BALANCE**
Acrylic, Paper
400 x 400 mm
Client/Special
Credits: El Búho

LA FLOR INFINITA Y SU FRUTO MARAVILLOSO
Acrylic, Paper
350 x 468 mm
Special Credits:
Antú Martín
Photography

020 / 021 **ROMANCE Y ANTÍDOTO**
Acrylic, Paper
210 x 298 mm

ROSAL
Acrylic, Paper
700 x 1000 mm

022 / 023 **FICTICIA NATURALIS**
Acrylic, Canvas
1000 x 1200 mm

LA ESENCIA DIVINA
Acrylic, Paper
310 x 450 mm

SENAKA SENANAYAKE

senaka-senanayake.com

Senaka Senanayake is a Sri Lankan artist who held his first international exhibition at the age of ten in New York. Although he has held many shows in his native country and abroad thereafter, it was only after he graduated in Art and Architecture from Yale University did he find his true calling. Upon moving back home, he began to delve deeper into its various environmental issues through his paintings.

024 / 025 **MIDNIGHT LOTUS BLOOM**
Oil, Canvas
4' x 4'

MY GARDEN
Oil, Canvas
5' x 4'

026 / 027 **GLORIOUS RAINFOREST**
Oil, Canvas
5' x 7.5'

029 **NATURE'S SYMPHONY**
Oil, Canvas
4' x 3'

030 / 031 **MORNING BLOOM**
Oil, Canvas
5' x 7'

MIROCOMACHIKO

mirocomachiko.com

mirocomachiko is a professional painter and author of children's books who was born in Osaka. She brings the natural world to life in her vivid style and has exhibited locally as well as abroad.

032 / 033

LILIUM LANCIFOLIUM
Acrylic Paint, Paper

PINK LEAF TREE
Acrylic Paint, Panel
910 x 727 mm

034 / 035

FLOWER NEXT RHAPHIOLEPIS INDIA VAR. UMBELLATA
Acrylic Paint, Panel
515 x 728 mm

DATURA
Acrylic Paint, Paper
500 x 650 mm

036 / 037

ANEMONE NARCISSIFLORA
Colouring Pencils, Acrylic Paint, Paper
513 x 363 mm

COSMOS
Colouring Pencils, Acrylic Paint, Paper
513 x 363 mm

LAURA GARCIA SERVENTI

lauragarciaserventi.com

Laura Garcia Serventi's work is inspired by her love of the botanical world as well as all of its wonders and oddities; often reflecting a combination of gardens and tropical landscapes that are connected to the memories of her childhood in South America. She established her brand ART and PEOPLE in 2012, and continues to work as a freelance illustrator on editorial and fashion collaborations.

038 / 039

RED TILED GARDEN
Gouache, Acrylics, Paper
558 x 711 mm

PINK TILED GARDEN
Gouache, Acrylics, Paper
360 x 460 mm

040 / 041

MONSTERA GARDEN
Gouache, Acrylics, Paper
360 x 460 mm

042 / 043

SPOTTED TROPICALIA
Gouache, Acrylics, Paper
558 x 711 mm

PASTEL TROPICALIA
Gouache, Acrylics on Paper
558 x 711 mm

044 / 045

BIRDS OF PARADISE
Gouache, Acrylics, Paper
760 x 1000 mm

TIFFANY KINGSTON

tiffanykingstonart.com

Tiffany Kingston creates artwork featuring the native habitats of Byron Bay. Originally from Melbourne, she trained as a graphic designer and operated a creative business for 15 years as a commercial mural artist and visual merchandiser before becoming a modern botanical artist. Her multilayered style is meticulously carved with primitive mark-making and expressed within a vibrant colour palette.

046 / 047

SOMETHING BEAUTIFUL
Acrylic, Canvas
900 x 900 mm

GODDESS
Acrylic, Canvas
1100 x 1100 mm

048 / 049

TEMPLE OF THE BLACK STAR
Acrylic, Canvas
1300 x 1100 mm

050 / 051

BLUE PLANET
Acrylic, Canvas
900 x 900 mm

AWAKEN
Acrylic, Canvas
2000 x 900 mm

WHOOLI CHEN

behance.net/whoolichen

Whooli Chen is a Taiwan-based freelance illustrator with years of professional experience. She works with a delicate colour palette and sensitive painterly layers that take her whimsical drawings to a whole new realm. Whooli has been involved in different fields, spanning across commercial illustrations and children's books.

052 / 053 A VASE OF FLOWERS
Pencil, Digital
215 x 297 mm
Client: Eslite Bookstore

FROM BLOSSOM TO FRUIT
Pencil, Digital
209 x 305 mm
Client: Newland Advertising

054 THE CURE
Pencil, Digital
231 x 297 mm
Client: China Times Newspaper

055 FOUNTAIN
Pencil, Digital
226 x 297 mm
Client: Wall Street Journal Magazine

056 / 057 CHILDREN'S BOOK 'STAR MOORING BAY'
Pencil, Digital
417 x 297 mm
Client: Parenting Publishing (Taiwan)

JULIA LUCEY

julialucey.com

Julia Lucey is a Fairfax-based artist whose inspiration stems from her years spent backpacking and working in the Western United States. As an Artist-in-Residence at Kala Art Institute, she has focused on traditional etching techniques and aquatint to create images dealing with the evolving issues of wildlife, its dissolution, and the attempt by many to direct its path.

058 / 059 GREAT EGRETS
Aquatint Etchings
1067 x 1067 mm

COMMON LOON UNDER THE MOON
Aquatint Etchings
762 x 610 mm

060 / 061 UNDERSTORY
Aquatint Etchings
915 x 762 mm

FOREST FOR THE TREES
Aquatint Etchings
1220 x 1372 mm

063 THE CROW AND THE HARE
Aquatint Etchings
915 x 610 mm

ROSA DE WEERD

rosadeweerd.com

Rosa de Weerd is a Dutch illustrator who focuses on flora and fauna. Her illustrations depict earthly subjects as well as otherworldly and peculiar plants, growing on undiscovered islands or faraway planets.

064 / 065 SPECIMEN NO.4 (RUBER APISCCOS)
Acrylic Paint, Wood
270 x 190 mm

SPECIMEN NO. 3 (RUBER LENTILAS)
Acrylic Paint, Ink, Wood
1100 x 750 mm

066 SPECIMEN NO. 2 (RUBER ALTALUS)
Acrylic Paint, Wood
230 x 130 mm

067 SPECIMEN NO. 6 (RUBER OSTREA)
Acrylic Paint, Wood
230 x 130 mm

068 / 069 FOLIO SPECIMEN NO. 1
Acrylic Ink, Dip Pen, Paper
210 x 148 mm

FOLIO SPECIMEN NO. 2
Acrylic Ink, Dip Pen, Paper
210 x 148 mm

ANDREA WAN

www.andreawan.com

Andrea Wan is a visual artist and illustrator who was born in Hong Kong, raised in Vancouver, and is now based in Berlin. Working mostly with ink on paper, her art combines traditional narrative aesthetics with eerie and surrealist qualities – depicting a world with great sensibility. She finds inspiration by looking outwards to observe her surroundings, as well as looking introspectively into the obscure corners of her sub-conscious.

070
/
071

INEVITABLE GROWTH
Ink, Paper Cutouts
300 x 400 mm

WONDERS
Ink, Paper Cutouts
300 x 400 mm

072 HORRIFYING BEAUTY
Ink, Paper Cutouts
400 x 500 mm

073 TOUCH
Ink, Paper Cutouts
400 x 500 mm

TIFFANY BOZIC

www.tiffanybozic.com

Tiffany Bozic is a California-based artist whose work has been described as 'John James Audubon on acid'. Her work evokes the tradition of tightly rendered illustrations that explode with highly emotional, surreal metaphors. Not so much departing from reality as articulating it more deeply, she establishes inescapable chains of consequence among the myriad species whose interactions create the world.

074
/
075

CURIOSITY
Acrylic, Maple Panel
24" x 24"

PHEROMONES
Watercolour, Paper
17" x 14"

076
/
077

CALLIGRAPHY
Acrylic, Maple Panel
20" x 14"

AGAPE
Acrylic, Maple Panel
36" x 48"

078
/
079

WHEN THE RAIN CAME
Acrylic, Maple Panel
Wood
54" x 24"

COMING TOGETHER
Acrylic, Maple Panel
72" x 36"

EDITH REWA BARRETT

edithrewa.com

Edith Rewa Barrett is an illustrator and textile designer based in Brisbane. With a fondness for the native flora of Australia, she seeks to share her sense of reverence for natural landscapes. Edith splits her time between commissions, exhibition work, and her eponymous label which features her illustrations on wearable and everyday goods.

080
/
081

LAMBERTIA FORMOSA
Pen, Digital, Paper
210 x 297 mm

KING PROTEA NIGHT
Pen, Digital, Paper
210 x 297 mm

082 THE COLLECTOR
Pen, Digital, Paper
297 x 420 mm

083 FAMILY PROTEACEAE
Pen, Digital, Paper
210 x 297 mm

084
/
085

WOOLLY STARS OF
THE LOWER BUSH
Pen, Digital, Paper
297 x 420 mm

THREATENED FLORA
OF THE OTWAYS
Pen, Digital, Paper
297 x 420 mm

ALICE
LINDSTROM

MARK CONLAN

MONIKA FORSBERG

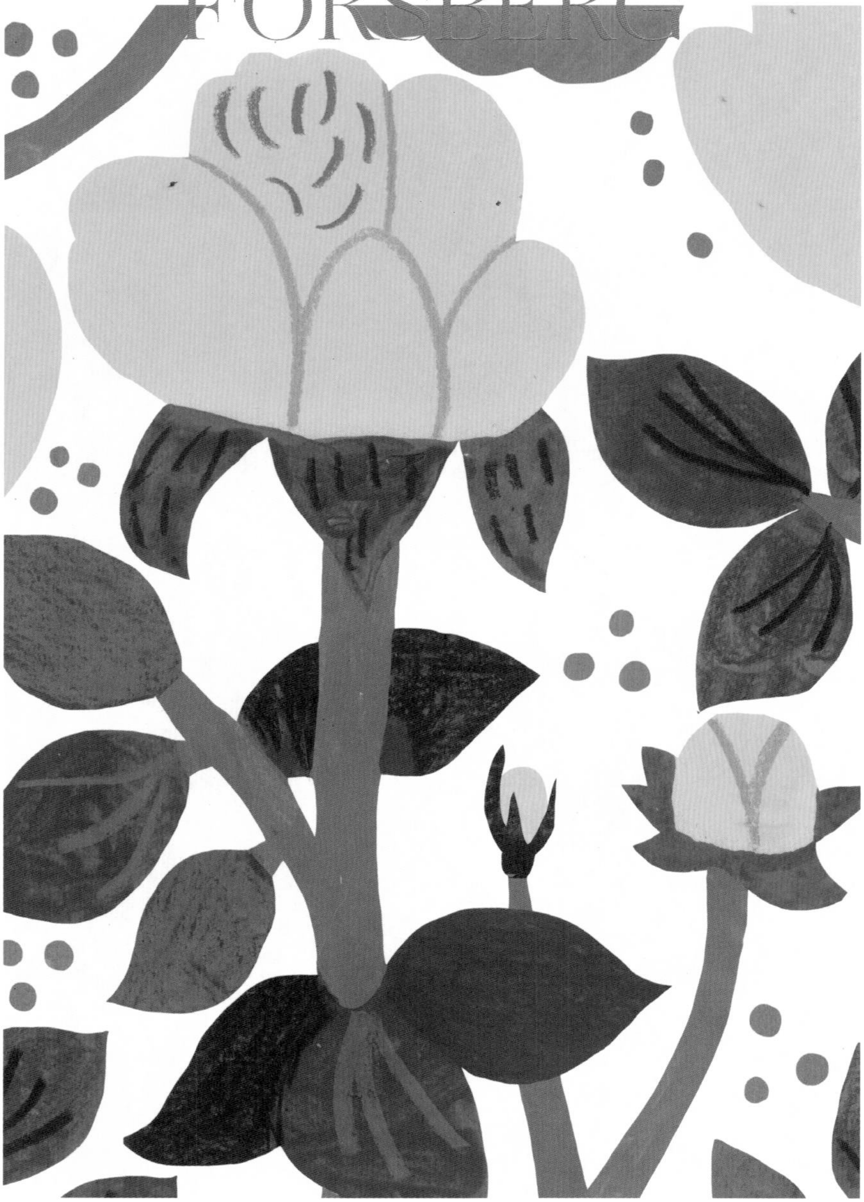

TAMAR DOVRAT

DANCELSTUDIO

LISEL
ASHLOCK

SARAH STRICKLAND

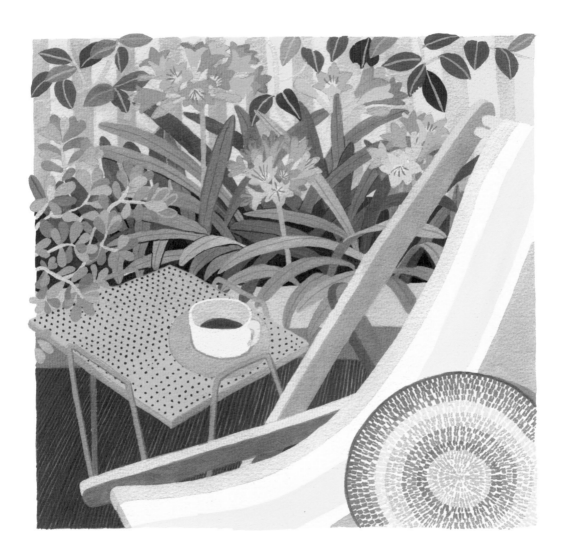

NATURE IN ART & ILLUSTRATION

FLORA
WAYCOTT

OLIWIA
EDYTA BOBER

Here we stand,
Like an Adam and an Eve,
Waterfalls,
The Garden of Eden,
Two fools in love,
So beautiful and strong,
The birds in the trees,
Are smiling upon them;
From the age of the dinosaurs,
Cars have run on gasoline,
Where, where have they gone?
Now, it's nothing but flowers.

Excerpt from '(Nothing but) Flowers'
by David Byrne
(Lyrics © Warner Chappell Music, Inc)

KARIN
MILLER

EMME
NORMA

1

2

3

4

CLOVER
ROBIN

Bluebell

Wild Sp
flo

Snowdr

Wood
anemone

coralroot

Primrose

wood
Sorrel

Lily-
of -the
walley

149

ALICE LINDSTROM
alicelindstrom.com

Alice Lindstrom's aesthetic stems from the diverse influences that continue to colour her life; spanning folk, mid-century, and modern movements in art and illustration. Armed with a background in philosophy, theatre design, museum studies, and art history, she creates textured and painterly paper collages that bring out the best in the medium and technique from her base in Melbourne.

090 / 091 **PAINTED VASE WITH WOMAN**
Painted Paper, Glue, Board
300 x 300 mm

STILL LIFE WITH FLOWERING GUM
Painted Paper, Glue, Board
300 x 300 mm

092 **THE RED FLOWERS**
Painted Paper, Glue, Board
300 x 300 mm

093 **STILL LIFE WITH TULIPS**
Digital Collage
210 x 250 mm

094 / 095 **LEOPARD IN THE GRASS**
Painted Paper, Glue, Board
200 x 280 mm

MARK CONLAN
markconlan.com

Mark Conlan is a multidisciplinary illustrator from Dublin who currently lives and work in Melbourne. His style and concepts focus on a strong use of character and composition empowered by whimsical and emotional situations. Incorporating rich and vibrant colour palettes, he aims to produce atmospheric imagery that surpasses the brief; often featuring happy little creatures or an array of plants.

096 / 097 **SEARCHING FOR EVE**
Digital
3508 x 4961 pixels

COME FIND ME
Digital
4000 x 6443 pixels

098 / 099 **VIETNAM DAY**
Digital
5000 x 4072 pixels

100 / 101 **ETSY WORLD OF ETSY SPOT ILLUSTRATION CHARMING GARDENS**
Digital
4200 x 1350 pixels
Client: Etsy

MONIKA FORSBERG
walkyland.com

Monika Forsberg was born and raised in a coastal city in the Swedish Lapland where 'it was almost always winter, yet the summers lasted forever'. She currently works as a freelance illustrator in London, and her style has been characterised as a mishmash of playful technicolour fantasies and rhythmical naivism.

102 / 103 **ROSE**
Paper, Ink, Pencil, Crayons
8" x 10"

PLANT
Paper, Ink, Pencil, Crayons
8" x 10"

104 / 105 **KEW GARDENS**
Paper, Ink, Pencil, Crayons
8" x 10"

LAGOM
Paper, Ink, Pencil, Crayons
8" x 10"

TAMAR DOVRAT
tamardovrat.com

Tamar Dovrat is an illustrator and pattern designer in Tel-Aviv who is inspired by the simplicity and complexities of nature. While her biggest love is gouache, she is often driven by the need to explore new methods and creative approaches. She enjoys the little pockets of beauty in everyday life that allow her to experience happiness, calmness, and excitement.

106 / 107

FLOWERS ON PEACH-PINK
Gouache, Paper
120 x 145 mm

FLOWERS ON GOLD
Gouache, Paper
110 x 170 mm

108

BIRDS AND FLOWERS – ART SERIES (1/4)
Limited Edition
Risograph Print
100 x 150 mm
Special Credits:
Risograph Print by
Dolce Press, Athens,
Greece.

109

SUMMER MINIS – FLOWERS ART SERIES ON SMALL FORMAT (NO.1)
Gouache, Paper
75 x 100 mm

DANCELSTUDIO
dancelstudio.com

DANCELSTUDIO is a print design and illustration studio based in Hamburg. Its work is inspired by various sources and characterised by the mixture of ideas from nature, travelling in tropical countries, as well as modern art and design in finding the symbioses between strong and whimsical elements to create unique outcomes.

110 / 111

ORANGES
Mixed Media
Max A4 (210 x 297 mm)

LEAVES
Mixed Media
Max A4 (210 x 297 mm)

112 / 113

JUNGLE PLANT
Mixed Media
Max A4 (210 x 297 mm)

MONSTERA
Mixed Media
Max A4 (210 x 297 mm)

114 / 115

PANSIES
Mixed Media
Max A4 (210 x 297 mm)

LEAF COLLECTION
Mixed Media
Max A4 (210 x 297 mm)

LISEL ASHLOCK
liseljaneashlock.com

Lisel Ashlock is a freelance illustrator who works in advertising, packaging, publishing, and design in Petaluma. Her acuity for botanical beauty and the natural world as well as her instantly recognisable style make her a sought-after talent for various projects; through which she offers a gleeful peek into the sacred wild.

116 / 117

DESERT HOUSE
Graphite, Paper,
Digital Colour
330 x 330 mm
Client: Visit Seattle
Magazine

SPRING FOOD
Graphite, Paper,
Digital Colour
406 x 508 mm
Client: The Washington
Post

118 / 119

LIVING ELEMENTS
Graphite, Paper,
Digital Colour
330 x 330 mm

SPRING FLORAL
Graphite, Paper,
Digital Colour
330 x 330 mm

SARAH STRICKLAND

sarahstrickland.com.au

Sarah Strickland is a textile designer and illustrator from the lush Dandenong Ranges on the edge of Melbourne who likes bold colour and hot tea. Her work focuses on finding the simple beauty in everyday life.

120 / 121
NATIVE POSY
Gouache, Paper
300 x 300 mm

BOWL OF APPLES
Gouache, Paper
330 x 420 mm

122
COLD TEA ON THE DECK
Gouache, Paper
300 x 300 mm

123
POTTING TABLE
Gouache, Paper
210 x 300 mm

124 / 125
A BIRD IN THE BUSH
Gouache, Wood Panel
400 x 290 mm

FLORA WAYCOTT

florawaycott.com

Flora Waycott is an English artist and illustrator who currently lives and works in Australia. Elements of nature, everyday objects, and tiny details are incorporated into her art with a dream-like quality; capturing inspiration from the small plants which live in her garden to travel and adventure in faraway places.

126 / 127
BLOOM
Gouache, Acryla Gouache
145 x 100 mm

MOTH DANCE
Gouache, Acryla Gouache, Digital
297 x 210 mm

128 / 129
DREAMS
Gouache, Acryla Gouache
260 x 185 mm

NIGHT GARDEN
Gouache, Acryla Gouache, Colouring Pencils
225 x 170 mm

OLIWIA EDYTA BOBER

oliwiabober.com

Oliwia Edyta Bober is a Polish-born illustrator who is currently based in the UK. She works primarily in gouache and occasionally explores the intricacies of paper-cutting. Drawing her influences from Polish folklore as well as her status as 'an immigrant in Brexit Britain', Oliwia's paintings often explore serious subjects veiled by a sea of beautifully coloured plants and geometric structures.

130 / 131
FOR DAVY
Gouache
297 x 297 mm

BATHROOM
Gouache
270 x 236 mm

132 / 133
FOLK TALES
Gouache
594 x 420 mm

135
HOURGLASS
Gouache
297 x 297 mm

KARIN MILLER

karinmiller.co.za

Karin Miller is intrigued by the magic charm and beauty of old botanical drawings as well as the subtle ambivalence brought about by their brilliant flawlessness while knowing of a plant's vulnerability. She reworks found images, photographs new elements, and draws to create work that is then printed in ink on paper. Through her chosen medium of collage, Karin explores the themes of harmony, tragedy, rhythm, and interruption.

136 / 137 **CRANACH VENUS WITH HARES**
Digital Collage
Various Sizes

DANCING JESUS
Digital Collage
Various Sizes

138 **VIRGIN IN THE ROSE GARDEN**
Digital Collage
Various Sizes

139 **VIGNAMAGGIO GARDEN**
Digital Collage, Ink Print
Various Sizes
Client: Villa Vignamaggio

140 / 141 **LIFE IN DETAIL: HOOKER GREEN**
Digital Collage
Various Sizes

BEHOLD THE LILIES
Digital Collage
Various Sizes

EMME NORMA

instagram.com/emilysteltenc2ce

Emme Norma has been working as a freelance illustrator since 2015. She enjoys drawing plants and botanical scenes; getting her inspiration from walking in the green countryside or travelling since she lives in the middle of the city in Düsseldorf.

142 / 143 **CRASPEDIA AND WHEAT**
Digital
148 x 210 mm

SUMMER MEADOW
Digital
297 x 420 mm

144 **(1) SNOWDROPS**
Digital
297 x 420 mm

(2) WILD FLOWERS VASE
Digital
210 x 297 mm

(3) WILD FLOWERS
Digital
210 x 297 mm

(4) FLOWERBOUQUET SUMMER
Digital
210 x 297 mm

145 **GREEN LEAVES**
Digital
297 x 420 mm

CLOVER ROBIN

cloverrobin.com

Clover Robin is a collage artist and illustrator who delights in nature and all things botanical. Inspired by a childhood filled with woodland walks and countryside rambles, she continues to illustrate for children's books and the occasional editorial. Clover currently lives and works in leafy Greenwich with her partner, Kev and cat, Winnie.

146 / 147 **TURNSTONES**
Handcut Painted Papers
297 x 420 mm

PUMPKINS
Handcut Painted Papers
230 x 250 mm

148 / 149 **WILD SPRING FLOWERS**
Handcut Painted Papers
210 x 297 mm

ANNA VALDEZ

MAYA HANISCH

AYANG CEMPAKA

TARA
LILLY

I wandered lonely as a cloud
That floats on high o'er vales and hills,
When all at once I saw a crowd,
A host, of golden daffodils;
Beside the lake, beneath the trees,
Fluttering and dancing in the breeze.

Continuous as the stars that shine
And twinkle on the milky way,
They stretched in never–ending line
Along the margin of a bay:
Ten thousand saw I at a glance,
Tossing their heads in sprightly dance.

Excerpt from 'I Wandered Lonely As A Cloud'
by William Wordsworth

173

GABY
D'ALESSANDRO

YUKI
KITAZUMI

AGATHE SINGER

I see trees of green, red roses too,
I see them bloom for me and you,
And I think to myself what a wonderful world.

I see skies of blue and clouds of white,
The bright blessed day, the dark sacred night,
And I think to myself what a wonderful world.

THOMAS HEINZ

JESS PHOENIX

I felt like lying down by the side of the trail

and remembering it all.

The woods do that to you,

they always look familiar, long lost,

like the face of a long-dead relative,

like an old dream,

like a piece of forgotten song

drifting across the water, most of all

like golden eternities of past childhood

or past manhood

and all the living and the dying and the heartbreak

that went on a million years ago

and the clouds as they pass overhead

seem to testify by their own lonesome

familiarity to this feeling.

Excerpt from 'The Dharma Bums'
by Jack Kerouac
(Copyright © Jack Kerouac. Published by The Viking Press, 1958.)

BJØRN
RUNE LIE

210

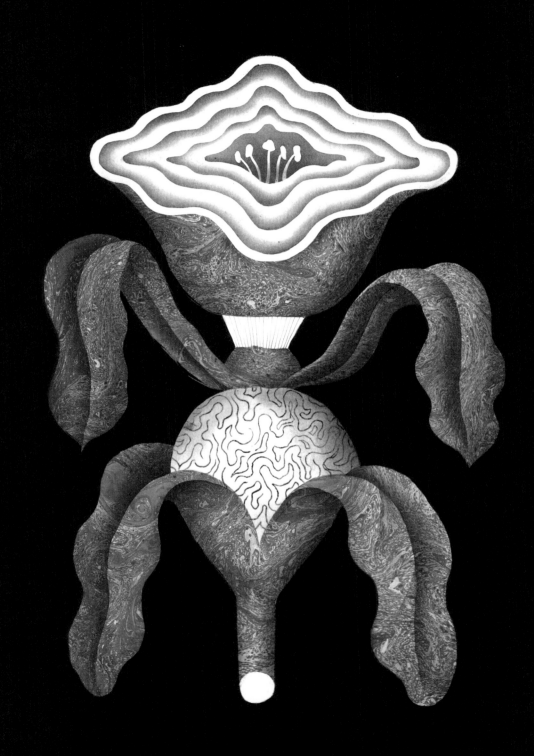

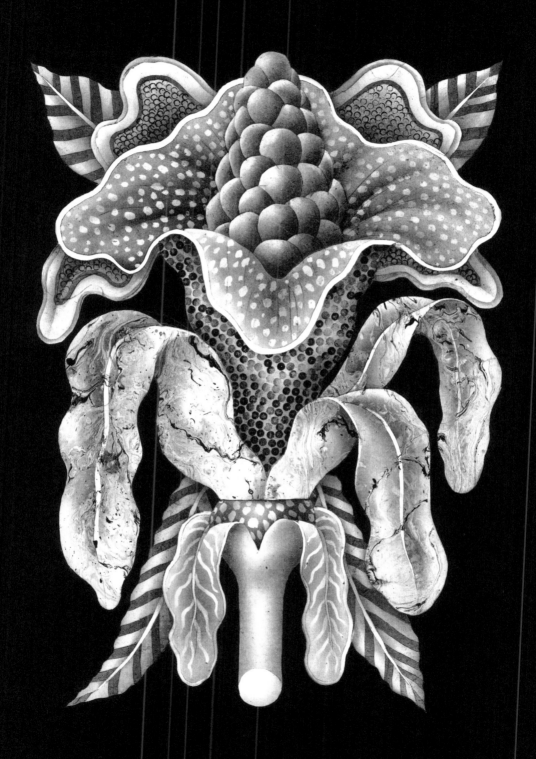

215

SASHA
FORTOVA

219

ANNA VALDEZ
www.annavaldez.com

Working across painting, drawing, printmaking, collage, and digital media, Anna Valdez examines the relationship between material and cultural identity, incorporating articles found in domestic spaces such as plants, textiles, vessels, and keepsakes into her work for storytelling. Her colourful pieces invite the viewer to consider objects as emblematic of personal and collective experiences.

154 / 155 TROPICAL VASE
Oil, Acrylic, Canvas
63" x 55"

VASES WITH
TROPICAL PLANTS
Oil, Acrylic, Canvas
52" x 48"

156 / 157 BROOKLYN VIEW
Oil, Canvas
42" x 54"

158 / 159 LANDSCAPE IN STUDIO
Oil, Acrylic, Canvas
66" x 84"

160 / 161 VENUS PAINTING
Oil, Canvas
84" x 66"

BROMELIAD WITH
DEER SKULL
Oil, Acrylic, Canvas
52" x 48"

MAYA HANISCH
instagram.com/maya_hanisch

Maya Hanisch is an artist and illustrator in Chile who has published several books in Europe, Latin America, the US, and the UK. A graphic design and painting studies graduate, she has won international recognition for her book 'Color Animal' and continues to have her artwork exhibited locally and abroad. Maya has also taught classes and workshops in various universities and book fairs around the world.

162 / 163 BOTANICAL 1
Acrylic, Paper
260 x 360 mm
Client: Quarto
Publishing

BIG BANG
Acrylic, Canvas
1600 x 1300 mm

164 / 165 FOLK PATTERN
Acrylic, Paper
260 x 360 mm
Client: Quarto
Publishing

LA JARDINERA,
VIOLETA PARRA
Acrylic, Paper
1202 x 2000 mm
Client: VD Magazine

AYANG CEMPAKA
behance.net/hellodaa0

Ayang Cempaka is an Indonesian artist and illustrator living in Dubai. She has been running a creative studio with her sister Asa since 2013, where she turns her childhood hobbies of drawing and making things into a range of well-crafted products. Ayang's work is characterised by its 'vintage-y' feel, vivid colours, as well as whimsical strokes.

166 / 167 ROSES
Digital
250 x 250 mm

FOREST FLORA
Gouache, Paper
297 x 420 mm

168 / 169 KEBUN (MY DAD'S
BACKYARD GARDEN)
Digital
420 x 520 mm

GARDENS BY THE BAY
Digital
320 x 440 mm

TARA LILLY

taralillystudio.com

Tara Lilly grew up on family farmland in rural Northern California surrounded by the redwood forest, open meadows, and the melodic sounds of birds singing. In addition to her love of nature, she is inspired by folk art, antique textiles, mid-century design, and her family. Tara enjoys painting everything floral, drawing charming characters, and exploring colour.

170 / 171

VIBRANT MOTH
Gouache, Paper
195 x 195 mm

MONARCH RESTING
Gouache, Paper
195 x 195mm

173

WILDFLOWER BOUQUET
Gouache, Paper
203 x 254 mm

174 / 175

DREAMY DAISY
Gouache, Paper
280 x 212 mm

FOLKLORIC FLORA BLUE & ORANGE
Gouache, Paper
192 x 115 mm

GABY D'ALESSANDRO

gabydalessandro.com

Gaby D'Alessandro is a New York City-based illustrator whose work has been recognised by American Illustration, Communication Arts, 3x3, and more. Her growing client list includes The New York Times, The Library of Congress, NPR, MTA Arts & Design, The Wall Street Journal, National Geographic Magazine, and The American Museum of Natural History.

176

THE SEEDS THAT SOWED A REVOLUTION
Digital, Pencil
346 x 254 mm
Client:
Nautilus Magazine
Art Direction:
Len Small

177

TAKE IT OUTSIDE
Digital
190.5 x 254 mm
Client: Teaching Tolerance Magazine
Art Direction:
Michelle Leland

178 / 181

ARRIVING IN NATURE
Digital
1095 x 212.7 mm
Client:
MTA Arts & Design

YUKI KITAZUMI

yukikitazumi.tumblr.com

Yuki Kitazumi is an award-winning illustrator based in Tokyo. A member of the prestigious Tokyo Illustrators Society (TIS), she works on book covers, magazines, newspapers, and picture books.

182 / 183

LEAVES
Paper Collage,
Acrylic Paint
280 x 280 mm

FLOWERS
Paper Collage,
Acrylic Paint
606 x 455 mm

184 / 185

MAGNOLIA
Paper Collage,
Acrylic Paint
297 x 206 mm

WEED
Paper Collage,
Acrylic Paint
410 x 282 mm

AGATHE SINGER
www.agathesinger.com

Agathe Singer is a French artist based in Paris. She creates illustrations for perfumeries, textiles, interiors, fashion, and publishing. Her work with gouache explores a universe of colourful flora, fauna, and strong women made of complex shapes, bright colours, and fiery movements.

186
/
187

A PIECE OF GARDEN
Gouache Painting
148 x 210 mm
Client:
Quatro Publishing
Special Credits:
Quatro Creates, Walter Foster Publishing

BLUE VASE
Gouache Painting
210 x 297 mm

188
/
189

JUNGLE
Gouache Painting
210 x 297 mm

191

BLUE PLANT ON BLACK
Gouache Painting
148 x 210 mm

192
/
193

BLUE PLANT ON CORAL
Gouache Painting
148 x 210 mm

GREEN PLANT ON YELLOW
Gouache Painting
210 x 297 mm

THOMAS HEINZ
neu.flachbild.de

Thomas Heinz is an artist, designer, and illustrator who currently lives and works in Cologne. His aesthetic features fluid shapes, bright patterns, and interesting colour combinations.

194
/
195

BLACK FLOWER
Pencil, Digital
300 x 400 mm

EYEFLOWERS
Pencil, Digital
300 x 400 mm

196
/
197

LEAVES AND DOTS
Ink Collage, Digital
300 x 400 mm

FLOWERS
Pencil, Digital
300 x 400 mm

198
/
199

TWO FLOWERS
Pencil, Digital
300 x 400 mm

SNAILFLOWER
Pencil, Digital
300 x 400 mm

JESS PHOENIX
jessphoenix.com

Jess Phoenix is a designer and illustrator in Seattle who specialises in making vibrant artwork and patterns. She uses floral imagery as a vehicle to explore colour – often making up the flowers and leaves as she goes along. Her work is hand-drawn but composed and coloured digitally.

200
/
201

SUNDAY
Marker, Paint, Digital
305 x 407 mm

GREENERY
Marker, Paint, Digital
305 x 407 mm

202
/
203

PRISM
Marker, Paint, Digital
305 x 407 mm

ANEMONE
Marker, Paint, Digital
305 x 407 mm

EDDIE PERROTE

eddieperrote.com

Eddie Perrote is a trained illustrator, designer, and animator living and working out of his studio in Brooklyn. His visual language comes from a background of printmaking, drawing, and painting; characterised by his love of abstraction, form, pattern, and bright colours.

204
/
205

SMALL POT
Gouache
295 x 451 mm

METAL 22
Gouache
297 x 451 mm

207

JOSE CUERVO BOX
Mixed Media
549.78 x 754.7 mm
Client: Jose Cuervo

208
/
209

JUNGLE LURKING
Mixed Media
320.38 x 209.97 mm

BJØRN RUNE LIE

bjornlie.com

Bjorn Rune Lie is a Norwegian illustrator and artist who lives in Bristol. Although botanical illustration remains a big inspiration, he is more interested in playing with bizarre shapes, beautiful textures, and strange atmospheres than any accurate representations of plants – much to the dismay of his wife Lindsey, who is a gardener/horticulturalist.

210
/
211

BUG BOUQUET
Charcoal, Digital
500 x 500 mm
Client: eeBoo
Art Direction: Mia
Gallson

RED FLOWERS
Charcoal, Digital
Art Direction: Gion
Capeder

212

MARBLE TULIP
Charcoal, Marbling
Ink, Indian Ink
200 x 300 mm

213

SINISTER
NIGHTBLOOM
Pastels, Stamps, Oil
Crayons, Marbling Ink,
Indian Ink
200 x 300 mm

214
/
215

SKUMMEL BLOMST
Charcoal, Digital
Client: Robotbutikken

OMNIVOROUS
ORCHID
Pastels, Stamps, Oil
Crayons, Marbling Ink,
Indian Ink
200 x 300 mm

SASHA FORTOVA

behance.net/sashafortova

Sasha Fortova explores a wide range of creative techniques from her base in Moscow, but focuses mainly on classic illustration and textile design patterns. In her artwork, she explores the 'slow living' approach and expresses her interpretations of it through botanic and animalistic elements.

216
/
217

TIGRO
Digital
Various Sizes

MONKEY
Digital
Various Sizes

218
/
219

NIGHT
Gouache, Acryla
Gouache, Digital
Various Sizes

MADONNA
Digital
Various Sizes

220
/
221

ESCAPE
Digital
Various Sizes

EIJA
VEHVILÄINEN

YU–HSUAN WANG

A chickpea leaps almost over the rim of the pot
where it's being boiled.
'Why are you doing this to me?'

The cook knocks him down with the ladle.
'Don't you try to jump out.
You think I'm torturing you.
I'm giving you flavour,
so you can mix with spices and rice
and be the lovely vitality of a human being.

Remember when you drank rain in the garden.
That was for this.'

Excerpt from 'Chickpea to Cook'
by Rumi, as translated by Coleman Barks

/ 58

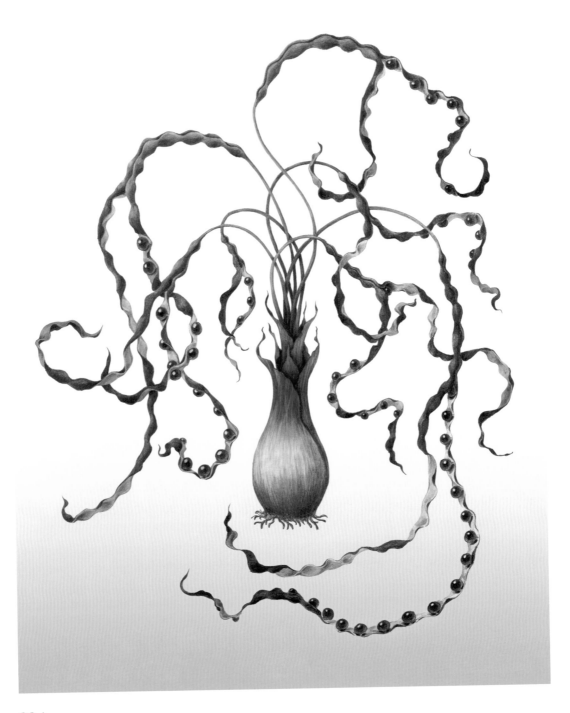

VICTORIA
CLARE GRAY

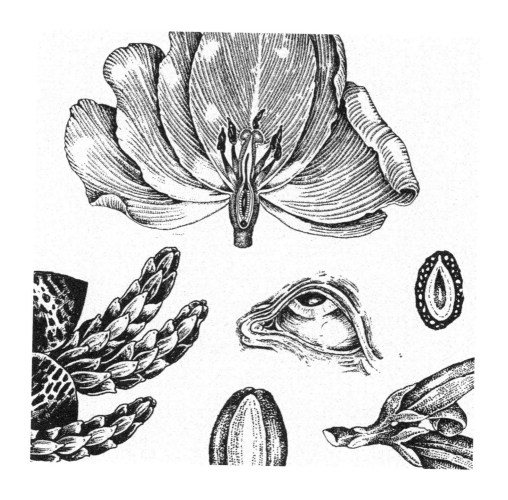

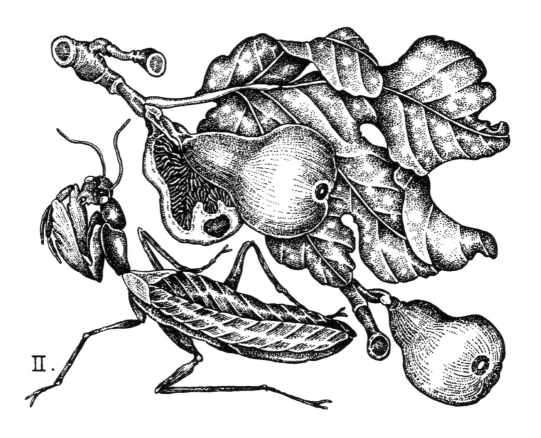

II.

LILI
ARNOLD

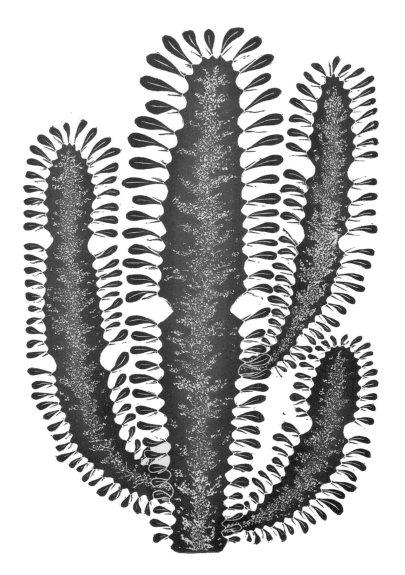

1/100   "Euphorbia Trigona"

5/100   "Echinopsis spectabilis" 2

243

E.V. 83/200   "Dos Saguaros"

"Echinopsis Mamillosa II"

DANA
KINTER

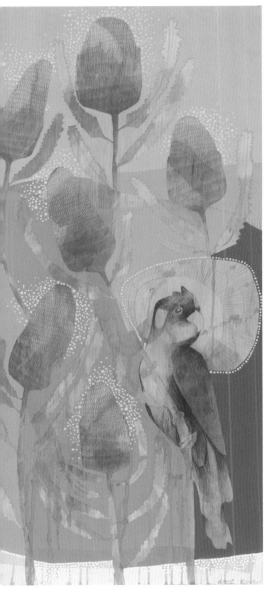

HANA
SEO

YUKO
KURIHARA

GABBY
MALPAS

263

265

There is another sky,
Ever serene and fair,
And there is another sunshine,
Though it be darkness there;
Never mind faded forests, Austin,
Never mind silent fields –
Here is a little forest,
Whose leaf is ever green;
Here is a brighter garden,
Where not a frost has been;
In its unfading flowers
I hear the bright bee hum:
Prithee, my brother,
Into my garden come!

'There Is Another Sky'
by Emily Dickinson

ANTONIN FAURE

269

FAURE 2014

273

MIZUKI GOTO

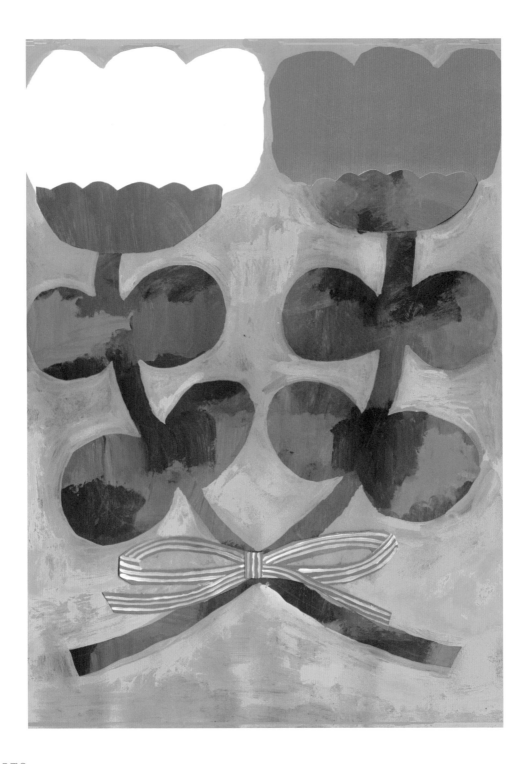

高さ4m
以上になる
草です。
樹ではあり
ません。本種
は日本・初導
入だそうです。
マダガスカル・
タンザニア
原産。

2015・1・30
チフォンドルム
リンドレヤヌム
Typhonodorum
Lindleyanum
サトイモ科

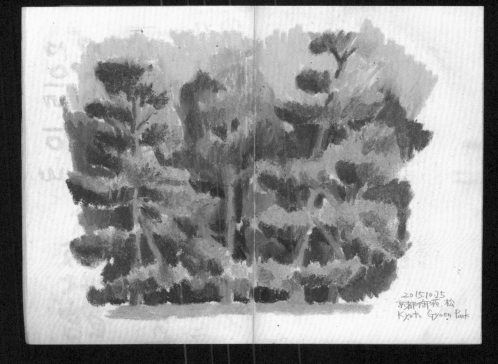

2015.10.25
京都御苑・松
Kyoto. Gyoen Park

2016.2.6
兵庫県
神戸動物王国
のんびりと
南国の植物
を描く。

途中、ナコツコ
がひとし
きり眺め
てから
くれー!

と言って
去っていた。
悔しかった
ようです。

花を初めて見た。
こんな美しい花だったのか!!

〇riental
paperbush

ミツマタの
名の通り・
枝は三ツに分かれ
て成長している。

京都 釈迦谷にて
2017.4・12

花道家、福井素心先生のお庭にて。

水仙に似た甘くて重い香り

うぶ毛

ミツマタ
三椏の花。

枝は和紙の素材として有名です。

花言葉は強靭、壮健、そして永遠の愛

BROMELIAS

KYO
BOTA
CAL
GA

京都
府立
物

アナナス館

EIJA VEHVILÄINEN
eijavehvilainen.com

Eija Vehviläinen is an illustrator from Helsinki whose style is organic, fun, and 'a little bit quirky'. Ever since graduating from Aalto University in Finland, she has been focused on drawing and painting – using bold colour combinations and defying gravity through her work for both print and digital purposes.

226 / 227   LILAC FLOWER
Gouache, Aquarelle Watercolour Pencil, Paper
280 x 380 mm

PEAR
Gouache, Aquarelle Watercolour Pencil, Paper
380 x 500 mm

228 / 229   CHERRIES
Gouache, Aquarelle Watercolour Pencil, Paper
380 x 500 mm

FUTURE RARITIES
Gouache, Ink, Paper
297 x 420 mm

YU-HSUAN WANG
yuhsuanwang.com

Yu-Hsuan Wang is a Taiwanese artist and graphic designer who studied and worked in Paris for years. Combining the elegant and the strange, her artwork is influenced by nature, animals, and plants; elements of which can be seen throughout her body of work.

230 / 231   JUNGLE FRUIT
Risography
297 x 420 mm

RAPHANUS
Risography
297 x 398 mm

233   FABACEAE
Risography
297 x 398 mm

234 / 235   FOOD FOR THOUGHT – HIANOLE
Pencil, Digital
297 x 420 mm

FOOD FOR THOUGHT – BABRINMAPH
Pencil, Digital
297 x 420 mm

VICTORIA CLARE GRAY
victoria-clare-gray.com

Victoria is an artist currently dwelling in the Lake District, UK. She has a keen interest in natural history, and is particularly fond of plants and insects. Her favourite materials are dip pen, ink, blue biro, and 0.5 mechanical pencils.

236 / 237   CRAWL UNDER
Pen, Ink
180 x 140 mm

SEED BLOOM
Pen, Ink
120 x 120 mm

STICKY FIG AND MANTIS
Pen, Ink
180 x 140 mm

238 / 239   DEAD GENTLE – CENTRAL AMERICA SPECIES
Pen, Ink
650 x 450 mm

LILI ARNOLD
liliarnold.com

Lili Arnold is a California-based artist and designer specialising in illustration, print-making, and textile design. What began as a study and representative expression of flora and fauna born from curiosity slowly morphed into a dedicated body of work over the years. With block-printing as her primary medium, Lili continues to explore the many wonders of the natural world.

240 / 241

242

EUPHORBIA TRIGONA
Relief Print
381 x 558 mm
(243)

ECHINOCEREUS PECTINATUS II
Relief Print
381 x 558 mm

PROTEA SUSARA
Relief Print
381 x 558 mm

243

PROTEA CYNAROIDES
Relief Print
381 x 558 mm

244 / 245

DOS SAGUAROS
Relief Print
381 x 558 mm

ECHINOPSIS MAMILLOSA II
Relief Print
381 x 558 mm

DANA KINTER
danakinterartdesign.com

Dana Kinter lives and makes in the wildlife-filled Fleurieu Peninsula of South Australia. Drawing from the natural environment surrounding her home as well as an Encyclopedia of Australian Birds handed down by her grandmother, she has created a signature style that embraces Australia's native flora and fauna.

246 / 247

RED EUCALYPTUS AND LITTLE THORNBILL
Mixed Media, Board
300 x 300 mm
Photography:
Chris Weverling,
Prolab Imaging

I AWOKE AND AT TIMES BIRDS FLED THAT HAD BEEN SLEEPING IN YOUR SOUL
Mixed Media, Board
900 x 900 mm
Photography:
David Summerhayes
Photography

248 / 249

FOUR SEASONS SERIES
- Spring – Laughing Kookaburra and Protea Repens
- Summer – Galah and Banksia Baxten
- Autumn – Yellow-tailed Blackcockatoo and Banksia Burdettii
- Winter – Australian Magpie and Yellow Kangaroo Tail

Mixed Media, Board
600 x 1200 mm
Photography:
Chris Weverling,
Prolab Imaging

250 / 251

WHEN IT IS DARK ENOUGH YOU CAN SEE THE STARS
Mixed Media, Board
1200 x 1800 mm
Photography:
Paul Atkins, Atkins
Photo Lab

HANA SEO
seohana.com

Hana Seo is a painter and illustrator based in Seoul. Her style is based on traditional Korean art, but her work tells stories about modern life.

252 / 253 DREAMS & TRAVELING
Pigment, Gold Leaf, Mulberry Paper
390 x 580 mm

254 / 255 THINGS
Pigment, Mulberry Paper
300 x 560 mm

YUKO KURIHARA
yuko-kurihara.com

Yuko Kurihara's unique style is rooted in traditional Japanese painting techniques. The Tokyo-based artist and illustrator expresses the beauty of plants by highlighting the shapes and patterns that indicate life; such as the holes on leaves left by insects, and the unruliness of growing roots. Besides drawing inspiration from the colours in nature, her work also celebrates their microscopic details.

256 / 257 VANDA
Mineral Pigment, Animal Glue
318 x 410 mm

SHELL GINGER
Mineral Pigment, Animal Glue
190 x 333 mm

258 POMEGRANATE
Mineral Pigment, Animal Glue
242 x 333 mm

259 BEETS
Mineral Pigment, Animal Glue
364 x 515 mm

260 / 261 THREE GORGONS
Mineral Pigment, Animal Glue
364 x 515 mm

PINEAPPLE
Pen
318 x 410 mm

GABBY MALPAS
gabbymalpas.com

Gabby Malpas is a New Zealand-born artist who has called Sydney her home since 2003 after living in the UK for 14 years. Her still-life images feature flora and fauna viewed and grown in Australia, with more than a hint of chinoiserie.

262 / 263 WINTER MAGNOLIAS
Watercolour, Pencil, Arches Paper
390 x 570 mm

ORCHIDS AND LEMONS IN A BLUE AND WHITE BOWL BY KEIKO MATSUI
Watercolour, Pencil, Arches Paper
390 x 570 mm

264 I WILL NOT LOVE YOU LONG TIME
Watercolour, Pencil, Arches Paper
760 x 560 mm

265 COLOURBLIND 2
Watercolour, Pencil, Canvas
1000 x 1400 mm

267 RANUNCULUS, ANEMONES AND CITRUS
Watercolour, Pencil, Arches Paper
390 x 570 mm

ANTONIN FAURE
antoninfaure.com

Antonin Faure mixes highly detailed compositions with finely crafted lettering to create his own aesthetic. After honing his skills at the School of Art and Techniques, he moved on to drawing storyboards and scenes in advertising and cinema before joining the renowned Gallimard Jeunesse publishing house to design book covers. Currently, Antonin works as an independent illustrator in Paris.

268
/
269

JUNGLE
Digital
297 x 210 mm

ATOCHA
Gouache,
Colouring Pencil,
Paper
420 x 297 mm

270
/
271

JUNGLE 2
Gouache,
Colouring Pencil,
Paper
500 x 650 mm

272
/
273

BOTANICAL ELEPHANT
Gouache,
Colouring Pencil,
Paper
500 x 650 mm

MIZUKI GOTO
zukkeenee.com/gallerymo-no.html

Mizuki Goto is an artist based in Tokyo. After graduating from Nagoya Designers College, she worked at a children's book store – an experience that continues to shape her career path to this day.

274
/
275

PHILADELPHIA
FLEABANE
Acrylic Paint, Paste,
Scissors, Varnish
420 x 297 mm

FLOWERS
Acrylic Paint, Paste,
Scissors, Varnish
420 x 297 mm

276
/
277

BOUQUET OF CROSS
Acrylic Paint, Paste,
Scissors, Varnish
364 x 257 mm

PERSIMMON
Acrylic Paint, Paste,
Scissors, Varnish
420 x 297 mm

STUDIO-TAKEUMA
studio-takeuma.com

Takeuma majored in graphic design at the Kyoto Institute of Technology before graduating in 2004, but eventually became skilful at conceptual illustrations depicting 'nonsense', light-hearted and dark humour. His love for sketching is evident in his bright style of expression.

278
/
279

KYOTO BOTANICAL
GARDENS
Oil Pastel
250 x 340 mm

KYOTO IMPERIAL
PALACE
Oil Pastel
340 x 250 mm

KOBE ANIMAL
KINGDOM
Oil Pastel
340 x 250 mm

280
/
281

EDGEWORTHIA
CHRYSANTHA
Tombow ABT
Pen, Liquitex Marker
Slim
260 x 190 mm

282
/
283

KYOTO BOTANICAL
GARDEN BROMELIAS
Tombow ABT Pen
260 x 190 mm

ACKNOWLEDGEMENTS

We would like to specially thank all the artists and
illustrators who are featured in this book for their
significant contribution towards its compilation.
We would also like to express our deepest
gratitude to our producers for their invaluable
advice and assistance throughout this project,
as well as the many professionals in the creative
industry who were generous with their insights,
feedback, and time. To those whose input was not
specifically credited or mentioned here, we also
truly appreciate your support.

FUTURE EDITIONS

If you wish to participate in viction:ary's future
projects and publications, please send your
portfolio to: submit@victionary.com